CHARLES SCHULZ

A Real-Life Reader Biography

Jim Whiting

Mitchell Lane Publishers, Inc.
P.O. Box 196
Hockessin, Delaware 19707

Printing   3   4   5   6   7   8   9

Real-Life Reader Biographies

Paula Abdul	Christina Aguilera	Marc Anthony	Lance Armstrong
Drew Barrymore	Tony Blair	Brandy	Garth Brooks
Kobe Bryant	Sandra Bullock	Mariah Carey	Aaron Carter
Cesar Chavez	Roberto Clemente	Christopher Paul Curtis	Roald Dahl
Oscar De La Hoya	Trent Dimas	Celine Dion	Sheila E.
Gloria Estefan	Mary Joe Fernandez	Michael J. Fox	Andres Galarraga
Sarah Michelle Gellar	Jeff Gordon	Virginia Hamilton	Mia Hamm
Melissa Joan Hart	Salma Hayek	Jennifer Love Hewitt	Faith Hill
Hollywood Hogan	Katie Holmes	Enrique Iglesias	Allen Iverson
Janet Jackson	Derek Jeter	Steve Jobs	Michelle Kwan
Bruce Lee	Jennifer Lopez	Cheech Marin	Ricky Martin
Mark McGwire	Alyssa Milano	Mandy Moore	Chuck Norris
Tommy Nuñez	Rosie O'Donnell	Mary Kate and Ashley Olsen	Rafael Palmeiro
Gary Paulsen	Colin Powell	Freddie Prinze, Jr.	Condoleezza Rice
Julia Roberts	Robert Rodriguez	J.K. Rowling	Keri Russell
Winona Ryder	Cristina Saralegui	**Charles Schulz**	Arnold Schwarzenegger
Selena	Maurice Sendak	Dr. Seuss	Shakira
Alicia Silverstone	Jessica Simpson	Sinbad	Jimmy Smits
Sammy Sosa	Britney Spears	Julia Stiles	Ben Stiller
Sheryl Swoopes	Shania Twain	Liv Tyler	Robin Williams
Vanessa Williams	Venus Williams	Tiger Woods	

Library of Congress Cataloging-in-Publication Data
Whiting, Jim, 1943-
    Charles Schulz/Jim Whiting.
       p. cm. — (A real-life reader biography)
    Summary: A biography of the creator of the popular "Peanuts" comic strip.
    Includes bibliographical references and index.
    ISBN 1-58415-131-5 (lib bdg)
    1. Schulz, Charles M.—Juvenile literature. 2. Cartoonists—United States—Biography—Juvenile literature. [1. Schulz, Charles M. 2. Cartoonists.] I. Title. II. Series
PN6727.S3 Z93 2002
741.5'092—dc21
[B]   2002023654

ABOUT THE AUTHOR: Jim Whiting has been a journalist, writer, editor, and photographer for more than 20 years. In addition to a lengthy stint as publisher of *Northwest Runner* magazine, Mr. Whiting has contributed to the *Seattle Times*, *Conde Nast Traveler*, *Newsday*, and *Saturday Evening Post*. He has edited more than 20 titles in the Mitchell Lane Real-Life Reader Biography series and Unlocking the Secrets of Science. He holds a B.A. degree in philosophy and an M.A. degree in English. He lives in Washington state with his wife and two teenage sons.
PHOTO CREDITS: cover: Shooting Star; p. 4 AFP/Corbis; p. 7 Bill Melendez; p. 18 Bettmann/Corbis; p. 21 Ted Streshinsky/Corbis; p. 26 Bill Melendez; p. 28 John Burgess/Getty Images
ACKNOWLEDGMENTS: The following story has been thoroughly researched, and to the best of our knowledge, represents a true story. While every possible effort has been made to ensure accuracy, the publisher will not assume liability for damages caused by inaccuracies in the data, and makes no warranty on the accuracy of the information contained herein.

Table of Contents

Chapter 1
A Big Risk

It was just a few weeks before Christmas in 1965, and Charles Schulz was worried.

Peanuts, the famous comic strip Schulz had begun in 1950, was now appearing every day in more than 1,000 newspapers. Most people in the country had become familiar with his characters: Charlie Brown, his dog Snoopy, grumpy Lucy, Schroeder with his piano, Linus with his security blanket, and the others.

Phrases he used in his cartoons such as "happiness is a warm puppy," "security blanket," and "good grief!" were in everyday use. Already collections of his best strips had been printed as books. Several books had also been written about him. *Peanuts* had even

The *Peanuts* comic strip was begun in 1950.

been featured on the cover of *Time* magazine a few months earlier.

But now he was going to try something different. The Peanuts gang was going to be on television. And no one knew if they would be as successful as they were in newspapers. In fact, if the television special was a failure, people might lose interest in the comic strip itself.

The idea had already met with some difficulties. When television director Lee Mendelson first proposed the idea of doing an animated special about Charlie Brown two years earlier, none of the TV networks was interested.

But when executives of Coca-Cola saw Schulz's picture in *Time* magazine, they wanted to sponsor a Peanuts special. And not just at any time of year, but at Christmas, the most popular holiday. There was just one catch: Since it was already close to the middle of the year, they had to see the basic plot outline soon. Very soon. Within two days.

So Schulz, Mendelson, and Bill Melendez, the man who animated Schulz's characters, went to work. They met that deadline. They then had only about four months to produce the entire show: the complete script, all the animated drawings,

In 1965, the Peanuts gang moved to television.

Bill Melendez is the animator who brought the Peanuts *characters to life.*

the musical score. After weeks of hard work, they met that deadline, too.

But then they ran into another difficulty. The CBS network had several objections. They said the action didn't move fast enough. They didn't like the musical score. They were afraid viewers would be put off because the climax comes when Linus quotes from the Bible. They suggested that maybe it should have a laugh track. They were so worried, in fact, that they even tried to prevent showing the program to a very important critic who normally previewed television shows.

And perhaps the biggest worry was about whose voices would be heard. Since Charles Schulz's words had always been on paper, they sounded different in everyone's head. People might feel let down if the characters' voices didn't sound how they had imagined them.

So Schulz and everyone else connected with the program had their fingers crossed when it was televised on the night of December 9. Would anyone even watch?

The answer was a resounding yes. *A Charlie Brown Christmas* was the second most popular program on television that week. More than 15 million people saw it. And it won an Emmy for the best network animated special.

That was just the beginning. Because of its success, nearly 50 more Peanuts specials were produced over the next 30 years. *A Charlie Brown Christmas* has become an enduring holiday classic, rebroadcast every year on television. Millions of families have purchased the video. Many have also bought the separate CD of the sound track, which made its composer, jazz pianist Vince Guaraldi, very famous.

The plot is actually very simple.

With the holiday approaching, Charlie Brown is becoming more and more frustrated. He's trying to understand what Christmas is all about as everyone around him seems caught up in materialism and bright lights. Finally he calls out in desperation: "Isn't there anybody who can tell me what Christmas is all about?"

And in one of the most memorable moments in television history, quiet Linus steps forward: "I can tell you, Charlie Brown. I know what Christmas is all about."

Everyone was worried. But, *A Charlie Brown Christmas* became an enduring classic and launched the way for 50 more *Peanuts* specials.

Chapter 2
A Shy Boy Named Sparky

Charles was an only child.

Charles Schulz was born on November 26, 1922, in Minneapolis, Minnesota. His parents were Carl and Dena Schulz. His father worked as a barber and his mother was a housewife. Charles would be their only child.

The little boy was only two days old when an uncle gave him the nickname of Sparky. That was short for Sparkplug, the name of a horse in *Barney Google*, a popular comic strip of that era. That nickname stuck with him for the rest of his life and was how he signed his first cartoons.

The family soon moved to nearby St. Paul, the other half of what is known as the Twin Cities. It didn't take the youngster long to discover his unique talent.

"My earliest recollection of drawing and getting credit for it is from kindergarten," he said. "The teacher gave us huge sheets of white paper and large black crayons. I drew a man shoveling snow, and she came around, paused, looked at my picture, and said, 'Someday, Charles, you are going to be an artist.'"

Apparently, that triggered something in him.

"It seems beyond the comprehension of people that someone can be born to draw comic strips, but I think I was," he said much later in his life. "My ambition from earliest memory was to produce a daily comic strip."

The following year he could draw a recognizable version of Popeye.

The young boy was close to both his parents, who, incidentally, didn't seem to have any obvious artistic talent. After school, Sparky would visit his father at the barber shop. He would wait quietly until his father was finished cutting people's hair. He would go over to the cash register, hit the No Sale key, then take out a nickel so that he could buy a candy bar. Father and son would walk home together, eat dinner with Dena, and then read comic strips in the newspaper and talk about them.

When he was two days old his uncle gave him the nickname "Sparky."

Schulz always had warm, fond memories of his early childhood.

"There are times," he wrote much later in his life, "when I would like to go back to the years with my mother and father. It would be great to be able to go into the house where my mother was in the kitchen and my comic books were in the other room, and I could lie down on the couch and read the comics and then have dinner with my parents."

Outside his family, he was somewhat shy. When he was in first grade, everyone in his class brought valentines to give to the kids they liked. Because he didn't want to offend anyone, he went with his mother the day before and picked out one for everyone. The next day, one by one, the kids got up, walked to the front of the class, and put their valentines into a large box on the teacher's desk.

"Classrooms are pretty big to a first-grader," he remembered as an adult, "and it was a long walk from where I sat to the front of the room. Everyone could watch you, and I couldn't do it. I took all the valentines home."

It was also evident that Sparky was very bright. He was named the outstanding boy student in second grade at the Richard Gordon Elementary School, and on two occasions after that was advanced half a grade. By the time he reached junior high, he was the smallest, youngest boy in his class.

"The roof fell in," he said later. His grades were horrible, he had pimples, and he didn't believe that anyone liked him—or even noticed him, for that matter. He became lonely and insecure—characteristics that *Peanuts* readers notice in Charlie Brown.

Another characteristic that readers notice is Charlie Brown's love for sports. That's also a reflection of Sparky's experiences. When he was growing up, there weren't any organized sports for youngsters such as Little League. So he and his friends would challenge the kids in other neighborhoods to games of baseball.

Because St. Paul gets very cold during the winter, there were always sheets of ice where the kids could skate and play ice hockey. They'd scrape the snow off the city streets and pile clumps of it to mark the goals. Often, they played hockey in street shoes instead of ice skates.

By the time he reached junior high, he was the smallest and youngest boy in his class.

Chapter 3
Hard Times

Charles sold his first drawing in 1937.

Charles Schulz wasn't exactly brimming over with confidence when he entered St. Paul's Central High School. He was skinny and didn't have many friends. A few years earlier, though, he had been given a dog, which he named Spike. In 1937, Spike was the subject of the first drawing Sparky sold. It was published in a popular newspaper comic strip called *Ripley's Believe It or Not!*

But not even that triumph could do much to raise his self-confidence. Even though he grew to be almost six feet tall and was a member of a golf team, he never had a date in high school. He never even asked anyone, because he didn't believe that any girl would want to go out with him.

And there was one final insult for the boy who believed that he was destined to draw. When he was a senior, he submitted a collection of his drawings to the high school yearbook. The yearbook editors didn't use a single piece of art by the boy who would eventually grow up to become the world's most famous cartoonist.

That rejection wasn't his worst memory of high school. By then, his mother had developed a painful cancer of the colon, or lower intestine. The family moved from their home to an apartment above a drugstore to make it easier for her to receive daily doses of pain-killing medication.

Dena, though, still looked out for her son. She found an ad for a school in Minneapolis, now known as the Art Instruction School, and wanted Sparky to enroll. The country was still caught in the Great Depression, which had begun a decade earlier, and there was little money. Somehow Carl Schulz managed to cut enough hair not only to support two employees and to put food on the dinner table (pancakes were a particular favorite), but also to pay the $170 tuition for his son.

The art school was a correspondence school, which means students would do their

During the Great Depression, Sparky took art classes at a corres-pondence school.

work at home and then mail it in. Sparky was so shy and insecure that, even though the school was just a few miles away, he still mailed in his assignments. He didn't do very well, either. He earned only a C in a class called "Drawing of Children."

World War II soon put a stop to his art school studies. He was drafted into the army in 1943. While he was in basic training, his mother died. He survived the war without being wounded, but his mother's death left him scarred. He said it was "a loss from which I sometimes believe I never recovered."

Schulz returned from World War II with only limited prospects. Then, somewhat unexpectedly, the art school he'd attended before the war offered him a job as an instructor. In addition, he had another job, lettering the cartoons for *Timeless Topix*, a publication produced by the local Roman Catholic church. That helped him to develop and expand his cartooning skills.

Then, in 1947, he had his first real taste of success: He sent some cartoons to the *Saturday Evening Post*, at that time one of the country's most popular magazines. The editors accepted one, paying him $40 for it.

At about the same time, Schulz began working on a series of cartoons that he called

> **World War II soon put a stop to his art school studies. He was drafted into the army in 1943.**

L'il Folks. The *St. Paul Pioneer Press*, his hometown paper, began publishing those on a regular basis, each week in the Sunday paper.

"It was a wonderful way to start," he recalled, "because I had to think of only three or four ideas each week and yet there was a schedule to which I had to hold, so I learned to think of ideas on schedule. It gave me a chance to develop my drawing and my creativity."

Success followed success, as he eventually sold even more cartoons to the *Saturday Evening Post.*

Feeling bold, Schulz went to the editor of the St. Paul paper and asked if his cartoon could appear more frequently. The reply was no. Then he asked for more money. Again, he was turned down.

So he said, "Well, perhaps I should just quit drawing it."

This time the answer was yes.

Schulz was surprised but not defeated. He bundled up all the cartoons he'd drawn for the *Pioneer Press* and began submitting them to syndicates, which act as middlemen between cartoonists and newspapers throughout the country. A syndicate markets material to many newspapers at the same time, so the artist can make more money.

In 1947, the *Saturday Evening Post* purchased one of his cartoons.

At first Schulz was turned down. Then in 1950, United Feature Syndicate, located in New York, liked what they saw. They invited Sparky to interview with them.

Charles Schulz worked for many years at the same drawing board he purchased at the beginning of his career for $23.00.

The interview went well, and Schulz signed a contract with them to produce a daily strip.

A hitch quickly developed. The syndicate couldn't use the name *L'il Folks* because two strips already in existence had similar names. One was *L'il Abner* and the other was *Little Folks.*

By then Schulz had named the characters he would use. The main one was Charlie Brown, after a man he'd worked with at the art school. Schulz suggested the titles *Charlie Brown* and *Good Ol' Charlie Brown.* The syndicate didn't like either one. They came up with their own name: *Peanuts.*

Schulz was horrified. He didn't like it at all.

"No one calls small children 'peanuts,'" he protested. Besides, he thought, readers would be disappointed to find that no one in the strip was actually named Peanuts.

But the syndicate had made up its mind.

Because he was an unknown young cartoonist, Schulz didn't have any choice. He gave in.

On October 2, 1950, history was made. The very first *Peanuts* strip appeared. A total of seven newspapers carried it. Schulz earned $90 for his first week as a syndicated cartoonist.

Schulz was horrified when he learned that United Feature Syndicate wanted to name his comic strip *Peanuts.*

Chapter 4
The Little Red-Haired Girl

The strip began with four characters: Charlie Brown, Patty, Shermy, and Snoopy.

The strip began with four characters: Charlie Brown, Patty, Shermy, and Snoopy. Snoopy was actually named Sniffy at first, but one day Schulz saw a comic book about a dog named Sniffy, so he had to change the name.

Over the years, other familiar characters would appear: Violet, Lucy, Schroeder, Linus, Pig Pen, Franklin, Peppermint Patty, Marcie, and Woodstock.

And the Little Red-Haired Girl.

Though Charlie Brown has a crush on the Little Red-Haired Girl, he never works up the courage to go over and sit next to her. Or call her. Or give her a valentine. Unlike all the other child characters, however, she never appears in person. Finally, just before the strip came to an end, Schulz shows her dancing with Snoopy. But she is just a silhouette.

To Sparky Schulz, the Little Red-Haired Girl was far more than just a silhouette. Just as

Charles Schulz illustrates a Peanuts *comic strip.*

his professional career began taking off, his personal life took a staggering blow. Not long before, he had begun dating Donna Johnson, a woman who worked in the accounting department at the art school. She had bright red hair. Schulz fell in love with her. He even asked her to marry him. But there was a problem: Donna was in love with two men at the same time.

Her parents liked the other man a little better. He was a fireman, so he had a steady job with a dependable income. A cartoonist didn't seem like the best source of support for a woman who hadn't yet turned 21. And Donna had known the other man since they had been in junior high school. She chose him.

"That broke my heart," Schulz said. "I can think of no more emotionally damaging loss than to be turned down by someone whom you love very much. It is a blow to everything that you are. Your appearance. Your personality."

She was married 19 days after *Peanuts* made its first appearance. Schulz was devastated and in some ways never completely got over her. In later life, though, they became friends. She was proud of the strips that featured the Little Red-Haired Girl, even though her own hair had long since turned silver.

Chapter 5
Success

Schulz's love life soon improved when he met Joyce Halverson, the sister of another person he knew at the art school. Joyce and Sparky were married in April 1951.

They soon had five children: Meredith, Charles M. (Monte), Craig, Amy, and Jill. Not surprisingly, the kids provided many ideas for their father's comic strip.

When Meredith was two, her parents bought her a toy piano. Schulz thought, why not have one of the kids in the strip play that same instrument? The character Schroeder had just come into the strip, so Schulz began drawing him with his toy piano (which usually had a bust of the famous composer Beethoven on it). The piano became Schroeder's defining characteristic.

Soon he met and married Joyce Halverson.

Then there was the time that the whole family was sitting around the dinner table, and daughter Amy seemed particularly noisy. Schulz listened for about 10 minutes, then asked her to be quiet. She silently picked up a piece of bread and put butter on it. "Am I buttering too loud for you?" she asked. That exact phrase soon found its way into the strip.

By that time the family had moved from Minneapolis to the area where Schulz would spend the rest of his life: the rolling northern California wine country not far from San Francisco. The family bought a 28-acre horse ranch and named it Coffee Grounds. Joyce oversaw construction of the house, a swimming pool, tennis courts, and even a four-hole golf course on the property.

Not long afterward, she also oversaw construction of a huge ice arena in the city of Santa Rosa, where Sparky could indulge his boyhood love of playing hockey. The Redwood Empire Ice Arena opened in 1969.

The year 1966 was not a good one for Schulz. His studio burned down. After it had been remodeled, Carl Schulz died there while visiting his son.

And those weren't the only setbacks. Schulz's marriage was coming apart. He and Joyce divorced six years later.

"The only surprising thing to me is that they stayed together so long, or that they married at all," said their daughter Amy, who was 17 at the time of the divorce. "They are nothing alike."

Schulz moved out of the house and began living by himself. Within a year he met Jeannie Forsyth, and they were married in 1973. He set up his drawing studio next to the ice arena and gave it one of the country's most distinctive and unique street addresses: 1 Snoopy Place.

Some newspaper editors thought that Schulz was putting too much emphasis on Snoopy. But Schulz disagreed. And unlike the time many years earlier when the syndicate made him change the name of his strip, this time Schulz won. There would be no changes.

One other thing would not change, either. Schulz never had anyone help him with the strip. Working by himself, he designed and drew every single panel of every single strip that appeared every day in newspapers around the world.

The Peanuts influence soon spread well beyond newspapers. Almost from the beginning, collections of strips were sold in book form. Then Peanuts datebooks and calendars appeared. Expanding far beyond

After Charles and Joyce divorced, he met Jeannie Forsyth, whom he married in 1973.

Sparky's wildest dreams, Peanuts merchandising soon included dolls, clothing, watches, toothbrushes, and much more. Later years would see videotapes, ice shows, and even CD-ROMs for computers.

All this, of course, made Charles Schulz a very rich man. In the mid-1990s it was estimated that he made more than $30 million every year. Not bad for a man whose first weekly *Peanuts* paycheck was less than $100.

A generous man, Schulz gave a lot of his money to worthy causes, such as the Jean

Charles Schulz (center) became so successful with his Peanuts *comic strip he earned a star on the Hollywood Walk of Fame. Bill Melendez is shown here with him (left).*

and Charles Schulz Information Center at Sonoma State University and the D-Day Museum in Washington, D.C. And he kept working, always working. He took a short vacation in 1990, but he spent most of it at his drawing board, trying out new ideas while newspapers reran old strips.

One night in November 1999, Schulz was taken to the hospital. His doctors discovered that one of the arteries in his abdomen was blocked. They also discovered something much worse: Schulz had an advanced case of colon cancer, the same disease that had killed his mother. To the shock and dismay of his fans around the world, Schulz had to announce his retirement. *Peanuts* had been a part of his fans' lives for so long that they couldn't bear the thought of it ending. Neither could Schulz.

His final daily strip appeared in January 2000. It shows Snoopy sitting on top of his doghouse in front of his typewriter, looking up as if for inspiration.

In 1999, doctors discovered that Schulz had a blocked artery and colon cancer.

"Charlie Brown, Snoopy, Linus, Lucy . . . how can I ever forget them . . . ," he reflects.

Just over a month later, on Saturday night, February 12, Charles Schulz died of a heart attack. By then it was early the next morning on the East Coast. Trucks filled with newspapers—containing the final *Peanuts* Sunday strip—were already rumbling out to begin their deliveries. As readers reached for the last original *Peanuts* strip ever to be published, they learned that its creator had just died.

Charles Schulz is seen here in November 1997 with his Peanuts *characters.*

Tributes began pouring in immediately. Many of Sparky's fellow cartoonists dedicated their strips to his memory. The airport near his home was renamed the Charles M. Schulz–Sonoma County Airport. An artist began creating an outdoor public sculpture of Charlie Brown and Snoopy to be placed in Santa Rosa's Depot Park.

The U.S. Congress awarded Schulz a posthumous Congressional Gold Medal. And he was honored with the National Cartoonists Society's lifetime achievement award. Even the Baseball Hall of Fame in Cooperstown, New York, paid tribute. They set up an exhibit called "You're in the Hall of Fame, Charlie Brown!" because nearly 2,000 *Peanuts* strips were about baseball.

The Charles M. Schulz Museum opened in 2002 in Santa Rosa to celebrate his life and accomplishments.

While we will never see Charlie Brown, Snoopy, Lucy, or Linus in any new adventures, more than 2,600 newspapers continue to reprint existing strips. Bookstores and libraries carry dozens of Peanuts collections. Most of the animated specials are readily available on videotape. The Peanuts crew is still very much alive in spirit.

Charles Schulz died the day before his final Sunday comic strip ran.

Selected Books by Charles Schulz

A Boy Named Charlie Brown (New York: MetroBooks, 2001).

A Flying Ace Needs Lots of Root Beer (New York: HarperHorizon, 1998).

Being a Dog Is a Full-Time Job (Kansas City: Andrews and McMeel, 1994).

The Charlie Brown Dictionary (New York: Random House, 1973).

Dogs Are Worth It! (New York: HarperPerennial, 1999).

Guess Who, Charlie Brown? (New York: Ballantine Books, 1992).

Happiness Is a Warm Puppy (San Francisco: Determined Productions, 1962).

How Romantic, Charlie Brown (New York: Ballantine Books, 1984).

I Told You So, You Blockhead! (New York: HarperPerennial, 1999).

I'm Not Your Sweet Babboo! (New York: H. Holt, 1992).

I've Been Traded for a Pizza? (New York: HarperHorizon, 1998).

It's a Dog's Life, Snoopy (New York: Ballantine Books, 2001).

It's Baseball Season, Again! (New York: HarperHorizon, 1999).

The Joy of a Peanuts Christmas (Kansas City: Hallmark Books, 2000).

Make Way for the King of the Jungle (Kansas City: Andrews and McMeel, 1995).

Nice Shot, Snoopy! (New York: Ballantine Books, 1982).

Peanuts Jubilee: My Life and Art with Charlie Brown and Others (New York: Holt, Rinehart and Winston, 1975).

Peanuts Treasury (New York: MetroBooks, 2000).

Peanuts: A Golden Celebration (New York: HarperCollins, 1999).

Peanuts: The Art of Charles M. Schulz (New York: Pantheon Books, 2001).

Shall We Dance, Charlie Brown? (New York: HarperHorizon, 1999).

Who Was That Dog I Saw You With, Charlie Brown? (New York: Fawcett Crest, 1973).

The Wonderful World of Peanuts (New York: Fawcett, 1954).

The World Is Filled With Mondays (New York: HarperPerennial, 1999).

You Can't Win Them All, Charlie Brown (New York: Fawcett Crest, 1972).

You Don't Look 35, Charlie Brown! (New York: Holt, Rinehart and Winston, 1985).

You've Come a Long Way, Snoopy (New York: Fawcett Crest, 1976).

You've Got It Made, Snoopy (New York: Ballantine Books, 1983).

Chronology

1922, born on November 26 in St. Paul, Minnesota

1928, begins kindergarten, where a teacher praises his drawing

1936, enters St. Paul Central High School

1937, first published drawing, a sketch of his dog Spike, appears in newspaper feature *Ripley's Believe It or Not!*

1940, graduates from high school

1941, signs up for correspondence course in drawing

1943, drafted into U.S. Army; mother dies of cancer

1947, begins publishing cartoon called *L'il Folks* in *St. Paul Pioneer Press*

1950, sells *L'il Folks* to United Feature Syndicate, which changes the strip's name to *Peanuts*

1951, marries Joyce Halverson

1952, *Peanuts* begins appearing on Sunday comic pages

1958, Schulz and his family move to Sebastopol, California

1965, *Peanuts* appears on cover of *Time* magazine; TV special *A Charlie Brown Christmas* premieres

1966, Carl Schulz dies while visiting his son in California

1967, musical *You're a Good Man, Charlie Brown* opens off-Broadway

1969, Apollo X astronauts carry Charlie Brown into space with them; Redwood Empire Ice Arena opens

1972, divorces Joyce Schulz

1973, marries Jeannie Forsyth

1974, named grand marshal of Tournament of Roses Parade in Pasadena, California

1984, *Peanuts* is accepted by its 2,000th newspaper, giving it a place in *Guinness Book of World Records*

1986, inducted into Cartoonist Hall of Fame and receives Golden Brick award for lifetime achievement

1990, named a commander of arts and letters by the French government

1996, receives his own star on the Hollywood Walk of Fame

1999, announces retirement on December 14

2000, dies on February 12, the evening before his final Sunday strip appears

Index